KU-166-173

Renato Rudatis

Italian Specialities

Cookery Editor Sonia Allison

Series Editor Wendy Hobson

foulsham

Foreword

Italian cuisine is a favourite international cuisine, based as it is on the use of impeccably fresh ingredients, for the most part simple, woven together in an unpretentious arrangement of perfect harmony. It is in a class of its own with immense style, enviable chic and minimal frills. Yet it remains subtle, sophisticated and the most classic of all cuisines, emulated with enthusiasm worldwide in restaurants and in the home.

Contents

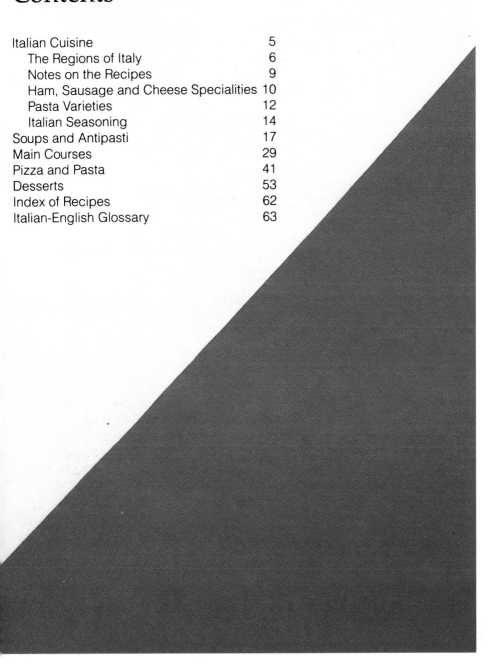

Italian Cuisine

Thinking of Italy, one can picture the delightful countryside, the sun and the sea, fresh fruits and vegetables and wonderful cooking. With a little guidance, recreating the best Italian dishes in your own home can be a pleasure.

The Regions of Italy

Trentino – South Tyrol

Trentino – South Tyrol is a double region, the two parts of which are administered separately. On the one side there is the German-speaking area of Bolzano, and on the other Trentino, a typical Italian city of culture. The area is characterized by glacier-crowned rocks, by rich soil and plenty of water.

The inhabitants of the area depend on mother nature for their bounty and their food tends to be robust and basic. In the Trentino area, pasta and simple meat dishes are common. Popular in the South Tyrol are soups, dumplings and pot roasts.

Veneto and Frinli

Veneto offers a little of everything: the Dolomite mountains, the Adriatic sea, the lakes at Gardia, spas and any number of cultural cities, with the capital Venice towering above them all. The region makes its living from intensively farmed land, producing mostly cereals and wine. According to an unwritten rule, the taste of any dish should not be adulterated; it must retain its own flavour. Pasta is something of a rarity in Veneto and more frequently one finds dishes of gnocchi, rice and polenta instead. The wines of this region are justly famous around the world.

Lombardy

This region shares its northern border with Tessin and Grabünden in Switzerland, stretching itself out on the plain of the river Po to the foothills of the Apennines mountains. It is the centre of Italian industry, commerce and banking. The capital is Milan, one of the largest and most lively crossroads in Europe, and often considered the true capital of Italy.

The inhabitants of Lombardy have the reputation of always being very busy, with little time to spare for the kitchen. They still love wonderful food, however, so typical dishes from Lombardy tend not to involve a lot of preparatory work in the kitchen.

Piedmont and Val d'Aosta

Piedmont in the north borders the south of France and Switzerland and is a region of art, culture and fine food. Nothing here is stinted, the cooking is generous and every dish a masterpiece, fit for the most fastidious of gourmets. Garlic plays an important role in the cooking and polenta (cornmeal) and rice are eaten more than pasta. Other preferences are salads, raw vegetables and raw meat.

Liguria

This stretch of countryside is recognisable because of the pervading scent of rosemary, basil, sage and other herbs growing wild. It is said that Ligurian cooking is created in the vegetable garden, in window boxes on balconies, in the woods and in the olive groves.

The narrow strip of coastal land leaves little room for cattle rearing, so meat for cooking is provided by mutton, lamb, rabbit and poultry. Above all, Liguria is the land of fishermen and of fish. The mild climate is ideal for the cultivation of vegetables, many of which are used as a filling for ravioli and similar pasta dishes.

Emilia-Romagna

This region is blessed with valleys, hills, mountains and sea, agriculture, cattle rearing and fishing. It borders with Liguria, Lombardy, Veneto and stretches as far as the Adriatic. Here many favourite holiday resorts, such as Rimini or Cattolica are to be found. The sociability of the inhabitants is proverbial, along with an outstanding sense of beauty. Their cooking is said to have reached perfection and is rich, sumptuous and varied.

Tuscany

When one thinks of Tuscany, it is not only the harmony of the countryside that comes to mind but also Florence, the work place of Michelangelo and Giotto. The Tuscans use simple ingredients for their dishes, but always of the best quality, preparing them according to traditional methods and using a wide variety of herbs. They call their cooking coquettishly 'poor cooking' because of its largely rural origin, the lack of sauces and the large number of cereal products included. However, herbs, vegetables, meat, fish and bread are common place on every table and there is a generous feel to Tuscan cooking.

Umbria

Although the countryside of this region is quite barren, cultivation takes place and the produce is harvested whenever possible. Umbrian cooking relies, as in times gone by, on the spit and the grill. Only a very few elaborate dishes are known here; everything is utilised depending on what is in season and on what nature herself has to offer: mushrooms, truffles, olives, fruit and herbs. In Umbria olive oil heads the list of ingredients and is used not only in the preparation of food, but is also poured over a meal just before serving and often stirred into soups.

The Marches

South of Emilia-Romagna, along the Adriatic coast, lie the Marches, an exceptionally fertile region with a friendly climate that suits cattle rearing and agriculture. Here one can eat superb meals at almost every restaurant and there is a massive choice of pasta dishes with imaginative and rich sauces and fillings. There are also many meat dishes and sweet specialities that are typical of the region.

Latium

Rome, the Italian capital, is the central point of this region and is elegant and cosmopolitan with its own international restaurants serving exotic cuisine as well as traditional Italian restaurants and even Indian tandooris and fish and chips. Traditional Roman cuisine is still alive, however, in many of the traditional parts of the city and in no other region are pasta dishes prepared so quickly and so simply: pasta is eaten just with butter or sheep's cheese, garlic or olive oil, bacon and eggs or with cheese and pepper. Another popular dish is gnocchi. Also many meat dishes such as Saltimbocca and delicious roast lamb, emanate from this region.

Abruzzi and Molise

A very singular piece of equipment is still to be found in the kitchens of Abruzzian housewives – the chitarra, a series of metal cords stretched over a board, which vibrates noisily when plucked. It is used to produce thin noodle strips to serve with tomatoes, mutton or lamb ragout. Abruzzian dishes are available only here; despite their excellent flavour, they have not spread to other parts of Italy.

Campania

This region takes in the Bay of Naples, the Sorrento peninsula, the Amalfi coast and the islands of Capri and Ischia. Campania has been blessed with some of the most fertile soil in Italy and to the north and south of Naples, the volcanic earth is warmed by the sun and watered by many rivers, providing the area with an abundance of fruit, vegetables and cereals. The tomato is the region's most favourite food. Naples is celebrated as the birthplace of spaghetti with tomato sauce, and of pizza.

Apulia

This stretch of land hides many secrets, such as the fairy-tale trulli or stone buildings, underground frescoes and fantastic grottoes. Mystery surrounds the Apulian cuisine, too. The ground is barren and stony, and one seems to see only olive groves and herds of sheep. Nonetheless, Apulia is one of the richest agricultural areas in Italy and produces wheat, wine, olives, fruit, berries and herbs. The Apulian cuisine consists mainly of pasta, vegetable and fish dishes served simply with vegetables, bread and cheese.

Basilicata

Sun and stones dominate the scenery, and in the middle of this barren, mountainous landscape, lonely sheep graze alongside pigs. Cereals, vegetables and wine are grown everywhere possible but, like the landscape, the cuisine is sparing and modest. The inhabitants live mainly on bread, olive oil, wine, vegetables, cheese and pasta in all shapes and sizes. Meat is rarely eaten, although a number of excellent sausages are made in the region.

Calabria

Calabrian cuisine has the reputation of being hot: it is said to consist largely of chillies, followed by olives and aubergines. Pork is also well-loved and is made into ham, bacon and sausages. Offal is used for many regional dishes. Calabria has a coastline of around 780 kilometres so the choice of fish available is excellent.

Sardinia

The island of Sardinia has unique scenery with mountains of silver granite, scented woods, miles of rocky, grassy landscapes and welcome peace and quiet. Even large towns like Cagliari, Nuoro or Sasari remain refreshingly traditional and old values are treasured and respected by its proud inhabitants. The cuisine includes strong-tasting stews, grilled meat and fish dishes.

Sicily

Sicily is naturally beautiful and has been shaped by sun, volcanic stone and sea, plus the marks left by immigrants and conquerors. People from all over the world have left traces of their lives, their culture and their culinary heritage. At one time there was no rice in Sicily but the Arabs introduced it along with many other foods such as citrus fruits. The cuisine here is rich in pasta, fish and meat dishes, fruit and sweet desserts. Ice cream here is superb.

Notes on the Recipes

1 Follow one set of measurements only, do not mix metric and Imperial.
2 Eggs are size 2.
3 Wash fresh produce before preparation.
4 Spoon measurements are level.
5 Adjust seasoning and strongly-flavoured ingredients, such as onions and garlic, to suit your own taste.
6 If you substitute dried for fresh herbs, use only half the amount specified.
7 Kcals refer to one portion of the recipe and are approximate.
8 Preparation times refer to preparation and cooking and are approximate.

Ham, Sausage and Cheese Specialities

Prosciutto Crudo
Prosciutto crudo is a wonderful cured raw ham. The very best, 'prosciutto di Parma' is a world famous ham especially from upper Italy with an old tradition of production going back 2,000 years. For this ham only selected pigs from an established area can be used. The flavour of the ham can be savoured best when it is cut into very thin slices. It is recognisable by the seal burnt into it, depicting the crown of the dukes of Parma.

San Daniele Ham
This choice product from San Daniele in Friaul is very much like Parma ham and is made by a secret process. Its special characteristic is its shape; it looks like a guitar in silhouette.

Mortadella
This sausage tastes different in every Italian region, depending upon individual taste and the spices which are added. Mortadella is made from lean, finely minced meat, interspersed with tiny cubes of fat.

Milan Salami
This is made only from lean beef and pork with added salt and a unique blend of spices. It has a longer shelf life at room temperature than other sausages. The name salami in Italian means salted meat.

Parmesan (Parmigiano)
This aromatic, lightly-coloured hard cheese is made from cow's milk and is Italy's premier cheese. It is widely used, when grated, to sprinkle over cooked dishes or blend into them, and in northern Italy, pieces of Parmesan are served for dessert with nuts and grapes.

Mozzarella
This is a delicious soft cheese which is sold in sealed plastic bags containing a brine solution to keep it fresh. Most

Mozzarella is made from cow's milk, but the best, and certainly the most expensive, Mozzarella di bufala, is made from buffalo milk.

Pecorino
This hard sheep's milk cheese has a unique and distinctive taste. From the area around Rome comes Pecorino Romano, with a particularly piquant flavour, and from Sardinia comes the softer Pecorino Sardo.

Mascarpone
This soft cheese made from cream has a similar consistency to quark and is largely used for desserts, such as Tiramisu.

Occasionally it is used in sauces for pasta dishes.

Gorgonzola
This soft blue vein cheese is made from cow's milk. Gorgonzola classico has a piquant taste while Gorgonzola dolce latte, has a somewhat milder flavour.

Ricotta
Ricotta is more of a sweet cheese, and similar to Mascarpone, though blander. It is largely used for desserts and as filling mixtures for pasta such as ravioli.

Bel Paese
This is a medium-fat cheese, similar in consistency to processed cheese, but with a gentle yet piquant taste.

Pasta Varieties

Pasta is available in all shapes and sizes, both fresh and dried. Particular shapes are traditionally matched with specific sauces – usually the richer the sauce, the thicker or wider the pasta – but it is very much a matter of personal taste. Choose a good quality pasta and try out different combinations until you find your favourites. If you do not have the pasta mentioned in a recipe, simply use something similar.

Cannelloni
Large tubes, normally filled with meat or vegetable stuffing and cooked in a white or cheese sauce.

Conchiglie
The name means mussels, because these pasta shapes are pressed inwards to resemble mussels.

Ditalini
Smallsh pasta that look like a thimble, this is often used in soups.

Farfalle
These little pasta bows are popular with all kinds of sauces.

Fettuccine
Thee wide pasta strips are perfect with meaty sauces.

Fusilli
Fusilli are spiral-shaped noodles that look like little corkscrews.

Lasagne
Popular everywhere, the flat pasta sheets are used in Lasagna dishes, or rolled into tubes and used as a substitute for Cannelloni.

Maccheroni/Macaroni
This fairly thick tubular pasta is available long, short and in small, curvy pieces.

Pappardelle
These are wide pasta strips with wavy edges, similar to fettuccine.

Penne
A short, tubular pasta cut at an angle, the name means quill.

Ravioli
The most famous filled pasta, ravioli is square pockets sealed along the edges. In Italy ravioli is filled with meat, Ricotta, ham or egg mixtures.

Rigatoni
Similar to penne, rigatoni is a short, thick tube pasta with a ridged surface.

Spaghetti
The original form of pasta, this consists of long thin strips of pasta. It is available in many different lengths.

Tagliatelle
These narrow pasta strips are, usually rolled together into tiny nests.

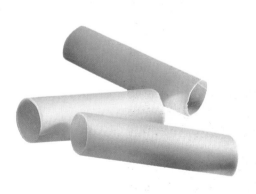

Tortellini

Rounded pasta pockets, usually filled with a mixture of meat, Mortadella and cheese, these are available fresh in many supermarkets.

Tortelloni

Also filled pasta pockets, these are somewhat larger than tortellini.

Vermicelli

This extremely thin spaghetti is used mostly in soups.

Cooking Pasta

'The guests must wait for the pasta and not the pasta for the guests.' This implies, correctly, that pasta should be cooked at the last minute and the time to allow will vary according to its shape and thickness. One golden rule is to cook the pasta only to the 'al dente' stage; tender but with a bit of bite still left in it. When overcooked, it becomes bloated and sloshy and to most tastes unpalatable. For best results allow 100 g/4 oz per person (for a main dish). Toss into a pan of lightly salted boiling water and boil, half covered or uncovered, until ready. A drop of oil added to the water will help to prevent the pasta from sticking together. Timing has to be judged by the cook, but as a general rule, small pasta needs about 5 minutes at most, medium pasta 8 to 10 and large pasta anything from 10 to 15 minutes. All pasta should be thoroughly drained before using. Fresh pasta will cook in just a few minutes.

Italian Seasoning

Olive Oil
Good olive oil can be recognised by its clear, light yellow to greenish colour and the best is extra virgin. It has a fine flavour and is free of saturated fat. Use in salad dressings and brief frying.

Grape Seed Oil
This is taken from the seeds of ripe grapes and is light and easily digestible. It has a mild yet distinctive flavour and is used largely in the south of Italy.

Garlic Oil
To make garlic oil, take olive oil or some other good quality oil and drop one or two peeled garlic cloves into it, according to taste. Leave for a few days before straining and using.

Balsamic Vinegar
Balsamic vinegar is an aromatic, deep red wine vinegar made from sweet Trebbiano grapes and matured for a long time (sometimes 50 years) in wooden barrels. Especially good balsamic vinegar comes from the region around Modena.

Herb Vinegar
Many Italians make their own herb vinegar to suit personal taste by adding a mixture of herbs and a dash of red wine or vermouth to wine vinegar. It is left to stand for a few days then strained into bottles with corks. Here, herb vinegar is readily available from most supermarket chains.

Red Wine Vinegar
In the making of red wine vinegar, as with white wine vinegar, only the best quality wine is used. The fermentation process takes place in wooden tubs filled with wood shavings. Until it matures the vinegar is stored in wooden barrels.

Marjoram and Basil
The special flavour of marjoram (left) refines meat dishes and sausage specialities and adds subtlety to soups and sauces.

Basil (right) is recognised by its smell. Fresh leaves have a warm and pungent flavour but dried basil tends to be blander. Buy fresh or chilled in tubs whenever possible.

Paprika and Peppers
In Italian cooking, it is usually mild paprika that is used and those who prefer a stronger, hotter taste, usually use chilli powder.

Freshly ground black pepper suits strong meat dishes, choose white pepper for white meat and fish foods and, when available, use freshly ground green peppercorns for pasta sauces.

Sage and Lemon Balm
The highly aromatic sage (left) is especially suitable for strong fish dishes and some types of Italian sausage are seasoned with it. A particular speciality is, however, fried sage leaves.

Lemon balm (right) has a very pleasant flavour, light and lemony.

Oregano and Coriander
Oregano (left) is top of the range in the Italian kitchen and there is hardly a pizza or combination of vegetables that does not contain oregano. It is very similar in its aroma to marjoram and is therefore sometimes known as wild marjoram.

Coriander (right) improves the taste of meat dishes, soups and salads.

Chilli Peppers and Garlic
These small pods have a distinctive peppery tone and should be added with caution to meat dishes and pasta sauces. Before using chillies, slit and remove the seeds which are very fiery. Wash the hands at once and avoid contact with eyes.

Garlic and Italian food are natural partners and garlic is said to aid good health.

Thyme and Rosemary
Thyme (left) is largely used to season meat and also fish dishes. The sweet sister of thyme, lemon-thyme, improves desserts.

Rosemary (right) has, just like basil, quite a strong flavour. The needles add a distinctive and unmistakable taste to meat, poultry, egg and mushroom dishes.

Soups and Antipasti

The first course in any meal takes the edge off the hunger pangs and should whet the appetite for the delightful dishes to follow.

Onion Soup, page 18

Onion Soup
Zuppa di Cipolla

Serves 4
Preparation time: 45 mins
350 kcal

450 g/1 lb onions, sliced

30 ml/2 tbsp olive oil

1 clove garlic, chopped

1 chilli pepper, chopped

15 ml/1 tbsp tomato purée

5 ml/1 tsp chopped fresh oregano

5 ml/1 tsp chopped fresh basil

150 ml/1/4 pt/2/3 cup dry white wine

750 ml/1 1/4 pts/3 cups stock

salt and freshly ground black pepper

a pinch of Cayenne pepper

a pinch of sugar

4 slices white bread

100 g/4 oz Mozzarella cheese, grated

1 Heat the oil and fry the onions lightly.
2 Add the garlic and chilli pepper and fry gently for a few minutes.
3 Stir in the tomato purée, season with the oregano and basil, add the wine and stock. Cover the pan.
4 Simmer the soup over a moderate heat for 25 to 30 minutes. Season well with salt, pepper, Cayenne pepper and sugar then pour into bowls. Add a slice of bread to each, sprinkle the Mozzarella on top and brown under the grill.

Photograph page 16

Broth with Toast and Egg
Zuppa Pavese

Serves 4
Preparation time: 25 mins
320 kcal

30 ml/2 tbsp olive oil

2 cloves garlic, chopped

4 slices white bread

750 ml/1 1/2 pts/3 cups stock

salt and freshly ground white pepper

a pinch of nutmeg

a pinch of Cayenne pepper

a pinch of sugar

4 eggs

5 ml/1 tsp vinegar

75 g/3 oz Parmesan cheese, grated

5 ml/1 tsp chopped fresh oregano

5 ml/1 tsp chopped fresh basil

1 Heat the oil and fry the garlic until transparent.
2 Place the white bread into the garlic oil and fry until golden on both sides. Lay the slices of bread into 4 deep bowls.
3 Heat up the meat stock and season well with salt, pepper, nutmeg, Cayenne pepper and sugar.
4 Poach the eggs in boiling water to which a little vinegar has been added. Remove, drain well and put one into each bowl.
5 Pour the hot meat stock around each egg and sprinkle with Parmesan, oregano and basil.

Photograph opposite (top)

Mussel Soup
Zuppa di Cocce

Serves 4
Preparation time: 45 mins
410 kcal

30 ml/2 tbsp olive oil

2 onions, diced

2 carrots, diced

1 small stick celery, diced

2 cloves garlic, chopped

salt and freshly ground black pepper

5 ml/1 tsp chopped fresh basil

5 ml/1 tsp chopped fresh oregano

10 ml/2 tsp grated lemon rind

250 ml/8 fl oz/1 cup dry white wine

700 g/7 oz canned tomatoes, chopped

1 1/2 kg/3 lb mussels, scrubbed and bearded

1 Heat the oil in a saucepan, add the vegetables and garlic and fry for 5 to 10 minutes until light gold.
2 Season with salt, pepper, herbs and lemon rind then add the wine and the tomatoes.
3 Add the mussels to the hot soup.
4 Cover the soup and cook over a moderate heat for about 10 minutes until all the mussels have opened. Season well before serving.

Photograph opposite (bottom)

Capricciosa Salad
Insalata Capricciosa

Serves 4
Preparation: 30 mins
425 kcal

1 iceberg lettuce, coarsely chopped

100 g/*4 oz* chicory, chopped

1 onion, diced

1 carrot, diced

1 red pepper, diced

100 g/*4 oz* mushrooms, sliced

juice of 1 lemon

100 g/*4 oz* cooked chicken breast, diced

100 g/*4 oz* tuna fish, flaked

100 g/*4 oz* Bel Paese cheese, diced

4 tomatoes, skinned and diced

100 g/*4 oz* black olives, stoned

45 ml/*3 tbsp* olive oil

100 ml/*3¹/₂ fl oz/6¹/₂ tbsp* balsamic vinegar

salt and freshly ground black pepper

1 Mix together the lettuce, vegetables, chicken, tuna and Bel Paese. Add the tomatoes and olives.
2 Whisk together the oil and balsamic vinegar and season with salt and pepper. Pour over the salad and toss lightly.

Photograph opposite (top)

Housewife's Salad
Insalata alla Cassalinga

Serves 4
Preparation time: 30 mins
515 kcal

1 lettuce, shredded

1 small head of chicory, separated into leaves

4 tomatoes, skinned and diced

1 red onion, chopped

100 g/*4 oz* white seedless grapes, halved

100 g/*4 oz* goats' cheese, cubed

100 g/*4 oz* ham, diced

2 hard-boiled eggs

50 g/*2 oz* anchovy fillets

90 ml/*6 tbsp* cold pressed olive oil

90 ml/*6 tbsp* balsamic vinegar

salt and freshly ground black pepper

1 bunch chives, chopped

1 Put the lettuce, chicory, tomatoes and onions into a bowl.
2 Add the grapes, cheese and ham. Cut each egg into 8 segments and add to the bowl.
3 Wash the anchovies, dab dry and add to bowl with rest of ingredients. Mix in olive oil, vinegar, salt and pepper and toss well to mix. Sprinkle with chives before serving.

Photograph opposite (centre)

Gourmet Salad
Insalata del bon Gustaio

Serves 4
Preparation time: 30 mins
490 kcal

2 onions, chopped

1 red pepper, chopped

1 green pepper, chopped

4 tomatoes, skinned and chopped

200 g/*4 oz* sheeps' cheese, cubed

100 g/*4 oz* black olives, stoned

90 ml/*6 tbsp* olive oil

90 ml/*6 tbsp* balsamic vinegar

salt and freshly ground black pepper

5 ml/*1 tsp* sugar

1 bunch chives, chopped

1 Mix the onions, tomatoes, cheese and olives in a bowl.
2 Mix in all remaining ingredients except the chives. Cover and put into the refrigerator for 10 to 15 minutes. Adjust seasoning to taste and sprinkle with the chopped chives before serving.

Photograph opposite (bottom)

Aubergines in Tomato Sauce
Melanzane con Salsa Piccaiola

Serves 4
Preparation time: 45 mins
390 kcal

2 large aubergines

10 ml/2 tsp salt

freshly ground black pepper

100 g/4 oz/1 cup flour

olive oil for frying

2 onions, chopped

4 cloves garlic, chopped

200 g/14 oz canned tomatoes, chopped

20 ml/4 tsp tomato purée

5 ml/1 tsp chopped fresh oregano

5 ml/1 tsp chopped fresh basil

150 ml/¹/₄ pt/²/₃ cup dry white wine

juice of ¹/₂ lemon

30 ml/2 tbsp fruit vinegar

a pinch of Cayenne pepper

a pinch of sugar

1 bunch chives, chopped

2 hard-boiled eggs, diced

30 ml/2 tbsp olive oil

1 Clean the aubergines, cut into medium-thick slices and transfer to a board. Sprinkle with salt and leave to stand for 30 minutes to extract as much moisture as possible.

2 Wash the aubergines then wipe dry. Season with salt and pepper and coat in the flour. Heat the olive oil in a frying pan, add aubergine slices and fry until golden, turning once. Remove from the pan then drain and arrange attractively in a dish.
3 For the sauce, fry the onions and garlic in the remaining olive oil until transparent.
4 Add the tomatoes and bring to the boil.
5 Stir in the tomato purée, sprinkle with oregano and basil and pour on the wine. Season well with lemon juice, fruit vinegar, Cayenne pepper, sugar, salt and pepper. Bring to the boil and then pour over the aubergine slices.
6 Sprinkle with the chives and eggs. Trickle the oil over the top and serve warm or cold.

Photograph opposite (top)

Gourmet Tip
This tomato sauce is also excellent for other types of vegetables. Watch the cooking time carefully for other types of vegetables: sliced mushrooms or courgettes can be fried for a short time in the sauce. Carrots on the other hand, must be boiled beforehand.

Marinated Courgettes
Zucchini Marinati

Serves 4
Preparation time: 45 mins
370 kcal

4 courgettes, sliced

salt and freshly ground black pepper

100 g/4 oz/1 cup plain flour

olive oil for frying

30 ml/2 tbsp olive oil

1 onion, chopped

2 cloves garlic, chopped

150 ml/¹/₄ pt/²/₃ cup vegetable stock

150 ml/¹/₄ pt/²/₃ fruit vinegar

150 ml/¹/₄ pt/²/₃ dry white wine

5 ml/1 tsp peppercorns

a pinch of sugar

2.5 ml/¹/₂ tsp chopped fresh basil

2.5 ml/¹/₂ tsp chopped fresh oregano

about 10 leaves of lemon balm, chopped

¹/₂ bunch parsley, chopped

1 Season the courgettes with salt and pepper.
2 Coat in flour and fry in hot olive oil until golden. Drain then arrange on a plate.
3 Heat the oil and fry the onion and garlic until soft.
4 Add the stock, vinegar, wine, peppercorns, sugar and herbs. Mix well, remove from the heat and pour the marinade over the courgettes. Cover and chill for 15 to 20 minutes before serving.

Photograph opposite (bottom)

Roast Veal in Tuna Sauce
Vitello Tonato

Serves 4
Preparation time: 40 mins
790 kcal

---

600 g/1 1/2 lb lean veal for roasting or turkey breast

2 cloves garlic

100 g/4 oz tuna fish

6-8 anchovy fillets

juice of 1 lemon

2-3 egg yolks

150 ml/1/4 pt/2/3 cup olive oil

250 ml/8 fl oz/1 cup double cream

75 ml/5 tbsp dry white wine

10 ml/2 tsp capers

salt and freshly ground black pepper

a pinch of Cayenne pepper

a pinch of sugar

---

1 Preheat the oven to 180°C/350°F/gas mark 4. Roast the veal or turkey for about 1 hour until cooked, then cool and chill. Cut into very thin slices and transfer to a plate.
2 Purée the garlic, tuna fish and anchovies.
3 Trickle in the lemon juice, egg yolks and oil.
4 Add the cream and wine and run the machine until mixture becomes a creamy sauce. Scrape into a bowl, stir in the capers and season with remaining ingredients.
5 Spread the tuna fish sauce evenly over the veal slices and refrigerate, uncovered, until well chilled.

Photograph (top)

Marinated Beef Fillet
Carpaccio

Serves 4
Preparation time: 30 mins
plus marinating
565 kcal

400 g/14 oz beef fillet
salt and freshly ground black pepper
15 ml/1 tbsp mild mustard
150 ml/¹/₄ pt/²/₃ cup dry white wine
75 ml/5 tbsp raspberry vinegar
juice of 1 orange
10 ml/2 tsp green peppercorns
2 cloves garlic, crushed
4-5 anchovy fillets, chopped
a pinch of Cayenne pepper
a pinch of sugar
5 ml/1 tsp chopped fresh oregano
2.5 ml/¹/₂ tsp chopped fresh basil
150 ml/¹/₄ pt/²/₃ cup olive oil

1 Cut the beef into very thin slices, season with salt and pepper then spread with mustard.
2 Mix the wine, raspberry vinegar, orange juice, peppercorns, garlic, salt and anchovy fillets.
3 Season with Cayenne, sugar, oregano, basil, salt and pepper. Stir in the olive oil a drop at a time.
4 Spread the marinade over the beef, cover and chill for 6 to 8 hours.

Photograph (bottom)

25

Baked Sardines
Sardine Fritte

Serves 4
Preparation time: 35 mins
905 kcal

16 fresh sardines

salt and freshly ground
white pepper

juice of 2 lemons

a dash of Worcester sauce

2 teacups breadcrumbs

75 g/3 oz Parmesan
cheese, grated

75 g/3 oz/³⁄₄ cup plain flour

2 eggs, beaten

olive oil for frying

1 lemon, cut into wedges

2 bunches parsley

1 Season the sardines with salt and pepper, sprinkle with lemon juice and a little Worcester sauce, then cover and leave to marinate in the refrigerator for 10 to 15 minutes.
2 Mix the breadcrumbs and Parmesan. Coat the sardines in the flour, then in eggs and then in the breadcrumbs mixture.
3 Heat the oil and fry the sardines until golden on both sides. Remove, drain well and arrange on a plate with lemon.
4 Fry the parsley quickly in the hot fat and use to garnish the dish.

*Photograph opposite
(top)*

Fried Squid Rings
Calamari Fritti

Serves 4
Preparation time: 45 mins
1210 kcal

750 g/1 ¹/₂ lb squid, ready-
to-cook

salt and freshly ground
white pepper

juice of 1 lemon

a few drops of Worcester
sauce

For the batter:

200 g/7 oz/1³⁄₄ cup plain
flour

2 eggs, separated

250 ml/8 fl oz/1 cup dry
white wine

sunflower oil for deep-frying

For the sauce:

250 g/8 oz/1 cup butter or
margarine

150 ml/¹/₄ pt/²/₃ cup dry
white wine

juice of 2 lemons

6 egg yolks

5 ml/1 tsp grated lemon rind

a pinch of Cayenne pepper

a pinch of sugar

1 Season the squid rings with salt and pepper, sprinkle with lemon juice and Worcester sauce and leave in the refrigerator for 10 to 15 minutes.
2 Meanwhile, sift the flour into a bowl, gradually add the egg yolks and wine and beat until smooth.
3 Whisk the egg whites until stiff and fold gently into the batter. Season with salt and pepper
4 Coat the squid rings in the batter and deep-fry in the hot oil until golden. Remove, drain well and keep warm.
5 For the sauce, melt the butter or margarine then cool to lukewarm. Mix the wine, lemon juice and the yolks together and beat until foamy in a basin standing over a pan of gently simmering water. Gradually whisk in the melted butter or margarine.
6 Add the lemon rind, then season well with salt, pepper, Cayenne pepper and sugar.
7 Arrange the squid rings in a dish and pour over the lemon sauce.

*Photograph opposite
(bottom)*

Main Courses

This selection of Italian dishes offers a range of superb meals to prepare for special occasions or to enjoy every day.

Veal in Cheese Sauce, page 30

Veal in Cheese Sauce, page 30

Veal in Cheese Sauce

Vitello al Uccelleto con Quadro Formaggio

Serves 4
Preparation time: 45 mins
670 kcal

---

600 g/1¼ lb veal fillet or chicken breast fillet

75 ml/5 tbsp olive oil

salt and freshly ground black pepper

a pinch of Cayenne pepper

1 onion, chopped

150 ml/¼ pt/²/3 cup dry white wine

150 ml/¼ pt/²/3 cup stock

150 ml/¼ pt/²/3 cup whipping cream

25 g/1 oz Bel Paese cheese, grated

25 g/1 oz Parmesan, grated

25 g/1 oz Fontina, grated

25g/1 oz Gorgonzola cheese, grated

1 little lemon juice

a pinch of sugar

½ bunch parsley, chopped

---

1 Cut the veal or chicken into thin strips. Heat the oil and fry quickly until light brown. Season with salt, pepper and Cayenne pepper. Remove from pan.
2 Add the onion and fry until transparent. Add the wine, stock and cream; stirring, bring to the boil.
3 Stir in the cheeses.
4 Season well with lemon juice and sugar and warm the meat in the sauce. Sprinkle with parsley.

Photograph page 28

Roman-Style Veal Escalope

Saltimbocca alla Romana

Serves 4
Preparation time: 30 mins
615 kcal

---

4 veal escalopes or chicken breast fillets, beaten flat

salt and freshly ground black pepper

a pinch of Cayenne pepper

4 slices lean bacon

8 sage leaves

75 ml/5 tbsp olive oil

150 ml/¼ pt/²/3 cup dry white wine

150 ml/¼ pt/²/3 cup stock

juice of 1 lemon

250 g/4 fl oz/1 cup cream

10 ml/2 tsp redcurrant jelly

30 ml/2 tbsp butter

a pinch of sugar

---

1 Season the meat with salt, pepper and Cayenne pepper.
2 Cover each piece with a slice of bacon and two sage leaves, fold together and secure with cocktail sticks.
3 Heat the oil, add the veal or chicken and fry until golden on both sides. Remove and keep warm.
4 Add the wine, stock, lemon juice, cream and redcurrant jelly to the pan.
5 Simmer gently, gradually whisking in knobs of butter. Season with sugar and pour over the meat.

Photograph opposite (top)

Liver in Wine

Fegato di Vitello alla Trentino

Serves 4
Preparation time: 30 mins
570 kcal

---

4 slices calves' or lambs' liver

salt and freshly ground black pepper

5 ml/1 tsp chopped fresh sage

75 g/3 oz/³/4 cup plain flour

2 cloves garlic, chopped

20 ml/4 tsp butter

100 g/4 oz smoked bacon, finely chopped

1 onion, chopped

1 leek, chopped

4 tomatoes, skinned and diced

150 ml/¼ pt/²/3 cup dry red wine

150 ml/¼ pt/²/3 cup stock

a pinch of paprika

a pinch of Cayenne pepper

a pinch of sugar

---

1 Season the liver with salt, pepper and sage and coat with flour.
2 Heat the garlic and butter, then fry the liver until cooked. Remove and keep warm.
3 Fry the bacon until gold. Add the onion and leek and fry until golden.
4 Add the tomatoes, wine and stock and simmer for 5 minutes.
5 Season with paprika, Cayenne and sugar and pour over the liver.

Photograph opposite (bottom)

31

Osso Buco Milan-Style

Osso Bucco alla Milanese

Serves 4
Preparation time: 2 hours
850 kcal

---

*4 thick slices shin of veal
with marrow bone*

---

*salt and freshly ground
black pepper*

---

100 g/4 oz/1 cup plain flour

---

150 ml/¹/₄ pt/²/₃ cup olive oil

---

1 onion, diced

---

100 g/4 oz celery, diced

---

2 carrots, diced

---

1 small leek, diced

---

3 cloves garlic, chopped

---

*10 ml/2 tsp grated lemon
rind*

---

45 ml/3 tbsp tomato purée

---

*200 g/7 oz canned
tomatoes, chopped*

---

*600 ml/1 pt/2¹/₂ cups dry
white wine*

---

2 bay leaves

---

*5 ml/1 tsp green
peppercorns*

---

5 ml/1 tsp juniper berries

---

a few cloves

---

1 sprig oregano

---

1 sprig basil

---

1 bunch parsley, chopped

---

1 Wash the veal under running water, pat dry, season with salt and pepper and coat with flour.
2 Heat the oil in a flameproof casserole, and add the veal and brown on both sides.
3 Add the onion, celery, carrots and leek and gently fry for about 10 minutes.

4 Add the garlic and lemon rind. Preheat the oven to 180°C/350°F/gas mark 4.
5 Stir in the tomato purée, tomatoes and wine. Add the bay leaves, peppercorns, juniper berries, cloves, oregano and basil. Cover the casserole, transfer to the oven and cook for 1¹/₂ hours.
6 Season the sauce with salt and pepper to taste. Arrange the veal slices on 4 plates, cover with the sauce, and serve sprinkled with parsley.

> **Gourmet Tip**
> Make a point of ordering veal shin well in advance as it is not always easy to come by and there is no substitute.

Neapolitan Pork
Braciole alla Napoletana

Serves 4
Preparation time: 1¼ hours
1065 kcal

---

4 pork chops

salt and freshly ground black pepper

2 cloves garlic, chopped

10 ml/2 tsp grated lemon rind

5 ml/1 tsp chopped fresh marjoram

5 ml/1 tsp chopped fresh sage

olive oil for frying

2 onions, chopped

1 red pepper, chopped

1 green pepper, chopped

100 g/4 oz mushrooms, coarsely chopped

200 g/7 oz canned tomatoes, chopped

250 ml/8 fl oz/1 cup dry white wine

8-12 rashers streaky bacon

1 Season the chops with salt and pepper. Preheat the oven to 180°C/350°F/gas mark 4.
2 Mix the garlic with the lemon rind and herbs and rub into the chops.
3 Heat the oil in a flame-proof casserole, add the chops and fry until brown. Add the vegetables and fry for 10 minutes.
4 Add the tomatoes and wine, cover and cook in the oven for 50 minutes.
5 Fry the bacon until crisp and arrange on top.

Photograph opposite (top left)

Florentine Beef
Vitello alla Florentina

Serves 4
Preparation time: 30 mins
670 kcal

---

4 beef fillets

salt and freshly ground black pepper

4 cloves garlic, crushed

10 ml/2 tsp grated lemon rind

5 ml/1 tsp chopped fresh oregano

2.5 ml/½ tsp chopped fresh basil

30 ml/2 tbsp fruit vinegar

150 ml/¼ pt/⅔ cup olive oil

5 ml/1 tsp paprika

1 red pepper, chopped

1 bunch parsley, chopped

1 Wash the beef under running water, pat dry and season with salt and pepper.
2 Mix the garlic with the salt, lemon rind, the herbs and fruit vinegar. Stir in the olive oil a drop at a time.
3 Mix in the paprika, pepper and parsley.
4 Spread the mixture equally over the beef fillets, cover and marinate in the refrigerator for 15 to 20 minutes.
5 Fry or grill the beef fillets until cooked to your liking.

Photograph opposite (top right)

Sunday Chicken
Polla della Domenica

Serves 4
Preparation time: 1¾ hours
690 kcal

---

1 large chicken

salt and freshly ground black pepper

10 ml/1 tsp chopped fresh oregano

2 cloves garlic

5 ml/2 tsp grated lemon rin

100 g/4 oz/1 cup plain flour

30 ml/2 tbsp olive oil

2 onions, chopped

2 carrots, chopped

1 stick celery, chopped

½ leek, chopped

1 bottle dry red wine

1 bouquet garni

a few cloves

a few green peppercorns

1 sprig rosemary

1 sprig thyme

1 Cut the chicken into and season with salt, per per and oregano. Mix th garlic and lemon rind an rub it into the chicker Preheat the oven 180°C/350°F/gas mark
2 Coat the chicken wi flour. Heat the oil an brown the chicken in flameproof casserole Add the vegetables an fry gently for 12 minute
3 Add all the remainin ingredients, cover an cook in the oven for 1¹, hours.

Photograph opposite (bottom)

Squid in a Pot
Calamari in Umido

Serves 4
Preparation time: 1 hour
330 kcal

---

600 g/1 ¹/₄ lb *squid rings*

---

30 ml/2 tsp *olive oil*

---

2 cloves garlic, chopped

---

2 onions, chopped

---

150 ml/¹/₄ pt/²/₃ cup dry
white wine

---

4 tomatoes, skinned and
chopped

---

400 g/ 14 oz canned
tomatoes, chopped

---

5 ml/1 tsp *chopped fresh
oregano*

---

5 ml/1 tsp *chopped fresh
basil*

---

10 ml/2 tsp *grated lemon
rind*

---

20 ml/4 tsp *tomato purée*

---

salt and freshly ground
black pepper

---

a pinch of Cayenne pepper

---

a pinch of paprika

---

a pinch of sugar

---

1 Wash the squid rings
under running water and
pat dry. Heat the oil, add
the squid rings and fry until very pale gold.
2 Add the garlic and
onions and fry for 3 min-
utes. Pour on the white
wine.
3 Add the tomatoes, season well with the remain-
ing ingredients, bring to
the boil, cover and simmer
until the squid is soft.

Photograph (top)

Grilled Lobster Tails
Scampi alla Griglia

Serves 4
Preparation time: 35 mins
630 kcal

12-16 lobster tails, shelled
75 ml/**5 tbsp** olive oil
5 ml/**1 tsp** salt
2 cloves garlic, crushed
5 ml/**1 tsp** chopped fresh oregano
5 ml/**1 tsp** chopped fresh basil
100 g/**4 oz**/¹/₂ cup butter or margarine
juice of 2 lemons
a dash of Worcester sauce
freshly ground white pepper
1 tea cup chopped mixed herbs

1 Wash the lobster tails well, drain thoroughly and transfer to a bowl.
2 Mix the oil, salt, garlic, oregano and basil. Spread evenly over the lobster tails. Marinate in the refrigerator for 10 to 15 minutes.
3 Heat the butter or margarine in a frying pan, add the lobster tails and fry briefly. Coat with the lemon juice, season well with Worcester sauce, salt and pepper then mix in the chopped herbs.

Photograph (bottom)

37

Trout in Tomato Sauce

Trota al Pomodoro

Serves 4
Preparation time: 1 hour
575 kcal

---

4 trout, filleted

juice of 1 lemon

a dash of Worcester sauce

salt and freshly ground
white pepper

75 g/3 oz/1¾ cups plain
flour

100 g/4 oz/½ cup butter

1 bunch spring onions

4 tomatoes, skinned and
diced

150 ml/¼ pt/⅔ cup dry
white wine

400 ml/14 oz passata

5 ml/1 tsp chopped fresh
oregano

5 ml/1 tsp chopped fresh
basil

a pinch of sugar

a pinch of Cayenne pepper

---

1 Sprinkle the trout with
lemon juice and Worces-
ter sauce, season with salt
and pepper and marinate
for 15 minutes.
2 Coat the fillets with flour
and fry in hot butter until
cooked through. Remove
and keep warm.
3 Cut the spring onions
into fine strips and fry until
transparent. Add the
tomatoes, wine and pas-
sata and season well with
the remaining ingredients.
4 Pour over the trout.

Photograph (top)

38

Palermo Sole

Sogliole alla Palermitana

Serves 4
Preparation time: 35 mins
685 kcal

---

8 sole fillets

5 ml/1 tsp lemon juice

a dash of Worcestershire
sauce

salt and freshly ground
white pepper

100 g/4 oz/1 cup plain flour

100 g/4 oz/½ cup butter

1 onion

2 carrots

2 sticks celery

150 ml/¼ pt/⅔ cup dry
white wine

juice of 2 oranges

juice of 1 lemon

200g/7 oz passata

50 g/2 oz/⅓ cup raisins
soaked in Marsala

50 g/2 oz/½ cup pine nuts

a pinch of Cayenne pepper

a pinch of sugar

a dash of wine vinegar

---

1 Sprinkle the fillets with
lemon juice, Worcester
sauce, salt and pepper
and marinate for 15
minutes.
2 Coat with flour. Heat the
butter and fry the sole until
cooked. Remove.
3 Cut the vegetables into
fine strips, then fry in the
butter until transparent.
4 Add the wine, orange
and lemon juice, passata,
raisins and pine nuts.
Bring the sauce to the
boil, season with remain-
ing ingredients and serve
with the fish.

Photograph (centre)

Mixed Seafood

Terrina di Pesce

Serves 4
Preparation time: 40 mins
580 kcal

---

800 g/1½ lb mixed seafood

salt and freshly ground
black pepper

5 ml/1 tsp lemon juice

a dash of Worcester sauce

20 ml/4 tsp olive oil

1 onion, chopped

2 carrots, chopped

1 stick celery, chopped

1 red pepper, chopped

1 green pepper, chopped

2 clove garlic, chopped

10 ml/2 tsp finely grated
lemon rind

400 g/14 oz canned
tomatoes, chopped

750 ml/1¼ pts/3 cups
vegetable stock

125 g/4 oz/⅔ cup sultanas

50 g/2 oz/½ cup pine nuts

a dash of wine vinegar

a pinch of sugar

100 g/4 oz Parmesan
cheese, grated

---

1 Clean and dice the sea-
food. Sprinkle with salt
and pepper and marinate
in lemon juice and Wor-
cester sauce for 30
minutes.
2 Heat the oil and fry the
vegetables until soft. Add
the garlic, lemon rind,
tomatoes and stock.
3 Add the sultanas, pine
nuts and the fish and simmer for 15 minutes. Sea-
son and sprinkle with
Parmesan.

Photograph (bottom)

Pizza and Pasta

The range of pizza and pasta recipes is limited only by the imagination of the cook – an ingredient which is rarely lacking in Italian cuisine.

Neapolitan Pizza, page 42

Neapolitan Pizza
Pizza Napoletana

Serves 4
Preparation time: 45 mins
plus rising
570 kcal

For the dough:
450 g/1 lb/2 cups strong plain flour
5 ml/1 tsp salt
10 ml/2 tsp sugar
1 sachet easy-blend dried yeast
15 ml/1 tbsp olive oil
300 ml/¹/₂ pt/1 ¹/₄ cups warm water
For the topping:
45 ml/3 tbsp tomato purée
4 tomatoes, skinned
4 hard-boiled eggs
100 g/4 oz cooked ham, cut into strips
50 g/2 oz anchovy fillets
50 g/2 oz black olives
salt and freshly ground black pepper
5 ml/1 tsp chopped fresh oregano
5 ml/1 tsp chopped fresh basil
200 g/7 oz Mozzarella cheese, sliced

1 Sift the flour and salt into a bowl. Stir in the sugar and yeast. Add the olive oil and water and work together to form a dough. If it is too dry, add a little more liquid; if too wet, extra flour. Knead thoroughly.

2 Transfer to an oiled bowl, cover with clingfilm and leave in a warm place for about 1 hour until the dough doubles in size.
3 Divide the pizza dough into 4 portions, roll out to fit 4 pizza plates and spread with tomato purée. Preheat the oven to 180°C/350°F/gas mark 4.
4 Cut the tomatoes and the eggs into slices and arrange evenly over the dough with the strips of ham.
5 Place the anchovy fillets and olives decoratively on top. Sprinkle with salt, pepper, oregano and basil, then add the Mozzarella slices.
6 Bake the pizzas for 25 to 30 minutes.

Photograph page 40

Mushroom Pizza
Pizza ai Funghi

Serves 4
Preparation time: 45 mins
plus rising
535 kcal

1 quantity pizza dough (p.42)
30 ml/2 tbsp olive oil
1 onion, chopped
50 g/2 oz smoked streaky bacon, diced
150 g/5 oz mushrooms, sliced
150 g/5 oz oyster mushrooms, sliced
salt and freshly ground black pepper
a pinch of Cayenne pepper
4 tomatoes, skinned and sliced
100 g/4 oz ham, cut into strips
200 g/7 oz Mozzarella cheese, sliced

1 Make the dough.
2 Heat the olive oil in a frying pan, add the onions and bacon and fry gently for about 7 minutes. Add the mushrooms and cook for a further 5 minutes.
3 Season the mushroom mixture to taste with salt and pepper. Place the rolled out pizza dough into 4 greased pizza tins and arrange the tomatoes and ham on top.
4 Spread the mushroom mixture on the pizzas and cover with slices of Mozzarella.
5 Bake the pizzas in the oven for 25 to 30 minutes.

Photograph opposite

43

Vegetable Calzone
Calzone di Verdura

Serves 4
Preparation time: 45 mins
plus rising
925 kcal

1 quantity pizza dough
(p.42)

30 ml/2 tbsp tomato purée

30 ml/2 tbsp olive oil

2 chicken breast fillets, cubed

salt and freshly ground black pepper

1 onion, chopped

1 red pepper, sliced

1 green pepper, sliced

1 courgette, diced

100 g/4 oz mushrooms, sliced

juice of 1 lemon

150 ml/¹/₄ pt/²/₃ cup dry white wine

5 ml/1 tsp chopped fresh oregano

5 ml/1 tsp chopped fresh basil

200 g/7oz Bel Paese cheese, grated

1 Make the dough. Roll it out into 4 rounds and spread with tomato purée. Preheat the oven to 180°C/350°F/gas mark 4. 2 Heat the oil in a pan. Add the chicken and fry for 5 minutes. Season with salt and pepper. 3 Add the vegetables and mushrooms. Sprinkle with lemon juice and pour in the wine. Season well, simmer for 5 minutes then cool.

4 Spread over one half of each of the rounds and sprinkle with herbs and cheese. 5 Fold each round over, press the edges well together and bake for 25 to 30 minutes.

Photograph opposite (top)

Foccaccia
Focaccia

Serves 4
Preparation time: 40 mins
plus rising
770 kcal

1 quantity pizza dough
(p.42)

2.5 ml/¹/₂ tsp aniseed

2.5 ml/¹/₂ tsp ground coriander

30 ml/2 tbsp olive oil

4 cloves garlic, sliced

100 g/4 oz stuffed olives, sliced

100 g/4 oz smoked bacon, cut into strips

1 Make the dough, adding the aniseed and coriander to the dry ingredients before adding the oil and water. 2 Place the dough into 4 greased pizza tins and brush with olive oil. Press the garlic, olives and bacon evenly into the dough and bake for about 20 minutes at 180°C/350°F/ gas mark 4.

Photograph opposite (centre)

Bolognese Pizza
Pizza alla Bolognese

Serves 4
Preparation time: 1 hour
plus rising
780 kcal

1 quantity pizza dough
(p.42)

30 ml/2 tbsp olive oil

400 g/14 oz minced beef

2 cloves garlic, crushed

1 onion, chopped

30 ml/2 tbsp tomato purée

400 g/14 oz canned tomatoes, chopped

a dash of red wine

5 ml/1 tsp chopped fresh oregano

5 ml/1 tsp chopped fresh basil

salt and freshly ground black pepper

45 ml/4 tbsp fresh breadcrumbs

4 tomatoes, skinned and sliced

200 g/7 oz Emmental cheese

1 Make the dough. 2 Heat the oil and fry the beef until brown. Mix in the garlic and onion. 3 Add the tomato purée, tomatoes and wine. Season with herbs, salt and pepper and simmer, covered, over a moderate heat for 25 minutes. Preheat the oven to 180°C/350°F/gas mark 4. 4 Place the pizza dough into 4 greased pizza tins, sprinkle with breadcrumbs and cover with tomatoes. Top with meat and sprinkle with cheese. Bake for 25 minutes.

Photograph opposite (bottom)

Baked Lasagne
Lasagne al Forno

Serves 4
Preparation time: 1¹/₂ hours
1095 kcal

30 ml/*2 tbsp* olive oil

400 g/*14 oz* minced beef

2 cloves garlic, diced

1 onion, chopped

1 carrot, chopped

100 g/*4 oz* celery, diced

1 leek, diced

30 ml/*2 tbsp* tomato purée

150 ml/¹/₄ pt/²/₃ cup dry red wine

400 g/*14 oz* canned tomatoes, chopped

5 ml/*1 tsp* chopped fresh oregano

5 ml/*1 tsp* chopped fresh basil

salt and freshly ground black pepper

a pinch of Cayenne pepper

5 ml/*1 tsp* paprika

For the béchamel sauce:

50 g/*2 oz*/¹/₄ cup butter

50 g/ *2 oz*/¹/₂ cup flour

300 ml/¹/₂ pt/1¹/₄ cups milk

300 ml/¹/₂ pt/1¹/₄ cups vegetable stock

15 ml/*1 tbsp* single cream

100 g/*4 oz* Parmesan cheese, grated

250 g/*9 oz* lasagne sheets

250 g/ *9 oz* Mozzarella cheese, sliced

1 Heat the olive oil in a pan, add the meat and fry briskly, stirring. Add the garlic and fry for 2 minutes.
2 Add the vegetables and fry for 5 to 7 minutes.
3 Stir in the tomato purée, wine and tomatoes.
4 Season the sauce well with oregano, basil, salt, pepper, Cayenne pepper and paprika. Simmer, covered for 25 to 30 minutes.
5 Meanwhile, make the béchamel sauce. Melt the butter in a pan, stir in the flour and cook gently for 2 minutes. Gradually blend in the milk and stock. Cook, stirring, until the sauce comes to the boil and thickens. Simmer, uncovered for 3 minutes.
6 Stir in the cream, a pinch of Cayenne pepper and the Parmesan cheese. Season well with salt and pepper.
7 Cook the lasagne sheets according to the instructions on the packet. Drain. Preheat the oven to 180°C/350°F/gas mark 4.
8 Grease an ovenproof dish and put in layers of the minced meat sauce, the béchamel sauce and the pasta sheets. Finish with béchamel sauce and top with slices of Mozzarella.
9 Bake the lasagne for 25 to 30 minutes.

Cannelloni
Cannelloni

Serves 4
Preparation time: 1½ hours
1255 kcal

30 ml/**2 tbsp** olive oil

300 g/**10 oz** minced beef

1 onion, chopped

250 g/**9 oz** spinach leaves, blanched and chopped

1 clove garlic, chopped

100 g/**4 oz** chicken livers, chopped

2 eggs

75 ml/**5 tbsp** single cream

100 g/**4 oz** Parmesan cheese, grated

salt and freshly ground black pepper

a pinch of Cayenne pepper

5 ml/**1 tsp** oregano

250 g/**9 oz** cannelloni

250 ml/**8 fl oz**/1 cup puréed tomatoes

½ recipe Béchamel sauce (page 47)

50 g/**2 oz** Pecorino cheese, grated

150 g/**5 oz** Bel Paese cheese, thinly sliced

1 Heat the oil in a pan, add the beef and fry briskly until well browned. Add the onion and fry gently for about 6 minutes.
2 Add the spinach and garlic and fry for 5 minutes. Transfer the mixture to a bowl.
3 Add the liver, eggs, cream and Parmesan. Mix well and season with salt, pepper, Cayenne pepper and oregano. Preheat the oven to 180°C/350°F/gas mark 4.
4 Prepare the cannelloni according to the instructions on the pack. Drain thoroughly.
5 Put the spinach mixture into a forcing bag with a large nozzle and pipe into the prepared cannelloni or spoon the mixture into the cannelloni. Place the filled rolls into a large greased casserole dish in a single layer.
6 Spread the tomato purée and the Béchamel sauce evenly over the rolls, top with cheese and bake for 20 to 25 minutes.

Photograph opposite (top)

Ravioli with Meat and Seafood Filling
Ravioli con Camberetti

Serves 4
Preparation time: 1 hour
1250 kcal

1 packet fresh lasagne sheets

For the filling:

100 g/**4 oz** cooked minced meat

200 g/**7 oz** peeled prawns

20 ml/**4 tsp** breadcrumbs

1 egg

1 cup chopped mixed herbs

50 g/**2 oz** Parmesan cheese, grated

salt and freshly ground black pepper

For the sauce:

20 ml/**4 tsp** olive oil

1 onion, chopped

30 ml/**2 tbsp** tomato purée

a little white wine

300 ml/**½ pt**/1¼ cups single cream

5 ml/**1 tsp** oregano

1 Cut the lasagne sheets into 4 cm/1½ in squares.
2 Mix together the ingredients for the filling and season with salt and pepper.
3 Spread a teaspoonful of filling on to each dough square. Moisten the edges, fold over and press lightly together.
4 Cook in salted water for about 12 to 15 minutes.
5 Heat the ol, add the onion and fry lightly. Add the rest of the sauce ingredients, season and simmer for 5 minutes. Drain the ravioli, put into a dish and coat with sauce.

Photograph opposite (bottom)

Spaghetti Bolognese
Spaghetti alla Bolognese

Serves 4
Preparation time: 1 hour
780 kcal

45 ml/**3 tbsp** olive oil
400 g/**14 oz** minced beef
3 cloves garlic, chopped
1 onion, chopped
2 carrots, chopped
1 stick celery, chopped
5 ml/**1 tbsp** tomato purée
150 ml/**¼ pt**/**⅔ cup** red wine
400 g/**14 oz** canned tomatoes, chopped
5 ml/**1 tsp** chopped fresh oregano
5 ml/**1 tsp** chopped fresh basil
salt and freshly ground black pepper
5 ml/**1 tsp** paprika
400 g/**14 oz** spaghetti
50 g/**2 oz** Parmesan cheese, grated

1 Heat the oil and brown the beef. Add the garlic and fry for 5 minutes. Add the vegetables and fry, stirring, for 10 minutes.
2 Mix in the tomato purée, wine and tomatoes.
3 Season well with the spices, cover and simmer for 40 minutes.
4 Cook the spaghetti in boiling salted water until al dente. Drain cover with the sauce and sprinkle with Parmesan.

Photograph opposite (top)

Chef's Special Tagliatelle
Tagliatelle dello Chef

Serves 4
Preparation time: 40 mins
720 kcal

400 g/**14 oz** tagliatelle
30 ml/**2 tbsp** olive oil
1 onion, chopped
250 g/**9 oz** mushrooms, sliced
juice of 1 lemon
100 g/**4 oz** ham, cubed
1 small tin peas, drained
a dash of white wine
250 ml/**8 fl oz**/1 cup single cream
salt and freshly ground black pepper
a pinch of Cayenne pepper
a pinch of sugar
50 g/**2 oz** Parmesan cheese, grated

1 Cook the tagliatelle in boiling salted water until al dente. Drain.
2 Meanwhile, heat the oil in a pan, add the onion and fry for 5 minutes.
3 Add the mushrooms and sprinkle with lemon juice. Add the ham and fry for 5 minutes.
4 Add the wine, peas and cream.
5 Season the sauce well with salt, pepper, Cayenne pepper and sugar and bring to the boil. Stir in the Parmesan, add the tagliatelle and heat through.

Photograph opposite (centre)

Farfalle with Mussels
Farfalle alle Vongole

Serves 4
Preparation time: 40 mins
650 kcal

30 ml/**2 tbsp** olive oil
2 cloves garlic, chopped
5 ml/**1 tsp** salt
1 bunch spring onions, cut into strips
6 tomatoes, skinned and diced
150 ml/**¼ pt**/**⅔ cup** dry white wine
450 g/**1 lb** cooked and shelled mussels
250 ml/**8 fl oz**/1 cup single cream
salt and freshly ground black pepper
a pinch of Cayenne pepper
a pinch of sugar
a dash of Worcester sauce
400 g/**14 oz** farfalle
1 bunch basil, chopped

1 Heat the oil, add the garlic and fry for 3 minutes. Sprinkle with salt.
2 Add the spring onion and fry until transparent. Add the tomatoes.
3 Mix in the wine, mussels and cream. Season with remaining ingredients and simmer for 10 minutes.
4 Cook the farfalle in boiling salted water until al dente. Drain thoroughly.
5 Add the basil to the sauce and spoon over the pasta.

Photograph opposite (bottom)

51

Splendid Desserts

The Italians create some wonderful desserts to round off any meal. Both traditional and innovative, they are all hard to resist.

Peach Pancakes, page 54

Peach Pancakes
(Crespelle con Pesche)

Serves 4
Preparation time: 30 mins
730 kcal

---
100 g/*4 oz*/1 cup plain flour
---
3 eggs
---
150 ml/*¹/₄ pt*/²/₃ cup milk
---
30 ml/*2 tbsp* sparkling mineral water
---
5 ml/1 *tsp* vanilla essence
---
10 ml/*2 tsp* grated orange rind
---
10 ml/*2 tsp* grated lemon rind
---
a pinch of salt
---
few drops of orange liqueur
---
25 g/1 *oz*/2 tbsp butter
---
4 fresh peaches
---
25 g/1 *oz*/2 tbsp butter
---
50 g/2 *oz*/¹/₄ cup caster sugar
---
150 ml/*¹/₄ pt*/²/₃ cup sweet white wine
---
30 ml/*2 tbsp* marmalade
---
a few drops of orange liqueur
---
75 g/3 *oz*/³/₄ cup pine nuts
---
4 scoops vanilla ice cream
---
sweetened whipped cream
---

1 Beat the first 9 ingredients.
2 Melt the butter and fry the pancakes.
3 Peel the peaches, remove the stones and dice the flesh. Heat the butter, add the sugar and heat until it caramelises.
4 Bring to the boil with the wine, stirring. Add the peaches, marmalade, liqueur and pine nuts. Simmer for 5 minutes.
5 Fill the pancakes with ice cream and peach mixture. Garnish with cream.
54

Red Wine Pears
Pera al Vino Rosso

Serves 4
Preparation time: 40 mins
445 kcal

---
8 small pears
---
juice of 1 lemon
---
15 ml/1 *tbsp* butter or margarine
---
75 g/*3 oz*/¹/₃ cup sugar
---
450 ml/*³/₄ pt*/2 cups red wine
---
1 vanilla pod
---
a few cloves
---
2 sticks cinnamon
---
30 ml/*2 tbsp* Maraschino liqueur
---

1 Peel the pears very thinly and sprinkle with lemon juice.
2 Heat the butter or margarine in a pan, add the sugar and let it caramelise.
3 Boil up the caramel with the red wine until dissolved. Add the vanilla pod, cloves and cinnamon sticks. Simmer over a moderate heat for 4 to 5 minutes.
4 Add the pears, cover and cook gently for 15 to 20 minutes.
5 Finally, remove the spices and flavour the liquid with Maraschino liqueur. Arrange the pears in a dish and pour over the red wine sauce.

Photograph opposite (top)

Photograph page 52

Baked Apples
Mele al Forne

Serves 4
Preparation time: 30 mins
630 kcal

---
4 Bramley apples
---
juice of 1 lemon
---
25 g/1 *oz*/¹/₄ cup pistachio nuts, chopped
---
25 g/1 *oz*/¹/₄ cup pine nuts, chopped
---
100 g/*4 oz* marzipan, softened
---
2 egg yolks
---
30 ml/*2 tbsp* single cream
---
75 g/3 *oz*/¹/₂ cup raisins soaked in rum
---
15 ml/1 *tbsp* butter
---
150 ml/*¹/₄ pt*/²/₃ cup white wine
---
150 ml/*¹/₄ pt*/²/₃ cup Marsala
---
30 ml/*2 tbsp* orange liqueur
---

1 Halve and core the apples and sprinkle with lemon juice. Preheat the oven to 180°C/350°F/gas mark 4.
2 Mix together the pistachio, pine nuts, marzipan, egg yolks and cream. Stir until smooth, then add the raisins.
3 Grease an ovenproof dish, add the apples and pour over the wine, Marsala and the liqueur. Bake for 15 minutes.
4 Spoon the marzipan mixture over the apples and bake for a further 6 to 8 minutes. Arrange the apples in a dish and pour over the sauce.

Photograph opposite (bottom)

Tiramisu
Tiramisu

Serves 4
Preparation time: 30 mins
plus chilling
570 kcal

4 egg yolks

75 g/3 oz/¹/₃ cup sugar

10 ml/2 tsp vanilla essence

*10 ml/2 tsp grated lemon
rind*

*300 g/11 oz Mascarpone
cheese*

a little lemon juice

*30 ml/2 tbsp Maraschino
liqueur*

*100 g/6¹/₂ oz/6¹/₂ tbsp
double cream, whipped*

12-16 sponge fingers

60 ml/4 tbsp Marsala

*cocoa and icing sugar for
sprinkling*

1 Put the egg yolks,
sugar, vanilla essence,
and lemon rind in a bowl
standing over a pan of hot
water. Beat until thick.
2 Mix the Mascarpone
with the lemon juice and
Maraschino until smooth.
Add the egg yolk foam
and the cream. Gently mix
all the ingredients.
3 Arrange the sponge fin-
gers over base of a serv-
ing dish and moisten with
Marsala. Spread over the
Mascarpone cream
evenly and sprinkle with
cocoa and icing sugar.
Cover and leave the des-
sert to chill in the refrigerator for at least 4 hours.

*Photograph opposite
(top)*

Zabaglione
Zabaglione

Serves 4
Preparation time: 30 mins
365 kcal

6 egg yolks

juice of 1 orange

150 ml/¹/₄ pt/²/₃ cup Marsala

5 ml/1 tsp vanilla essence

*30 ml/2 tbsp icing sugar,
sifted*

1 egg white

*75 g/ 3 oz/¹/₂ cup caster
sugar*

5 orange segments

4 marachino cherries

4 peach segments

1 Place the egg yolks with
the orange juice, Marsala,
vanilla essence and icing
sugar in a bowl over a pan
of gently simmering water.
Do not allow the water to
boil.
2 Beat with a whisk for
about 20 minutes until the
mixture becomes a thick
but light foam.
3 Take 4 stemmed
glasses, moisten the rims
with egg white then twist
in sugar.
4 Fill with the Zabaglione.
Spear the fruit on decora-
tive cocktail sticks and
use to garnish.

*Photograph opposite
(centre left)*

Ricotta Ice Cream
Gelato di Ricotta

Serves 4
Preparation time: 30 min-
utes plus freezing
690 kcal

5 egg yolks

100 g/4 oz sugar

10 ml/2 tbsp vanilla essence

*10 ml/2 tbsp grated lemon
rind*

*10 ml/2 tbsp grated orange
rind*

*10 ml/2 tbsp Maraschino
liqueur*

*25 g/1 oz/¹/₄ cup blanched
almonds, chopped*

*25 g/1 oz/¹/₄ cup walnuts,
chopped*

*25 g/1 oz/¹/₄ cup hazelnuts,
chopped*

*25 g/1 oz/¹/₄ cup pistachio
nuts, chopped*

*75 g/3 oz/¹/₃ cup glacé
cherries, chopped*

450 g/1 lb Ricotta cheese

1 Whisk together the egg
yolks and sugar until thick
and foamy.
2 Stir in the vanilla es-
sence, lemon and orange
rind and the maraschino.
3 Fold the chopped nuts,
glace cherries, and egg
yolk mixture into the
Ricotta.
4 Fill an ice cream mould
with the mixture, cover
and leave to freeze for 6 to
8 hours. Finally, remove
the ice cream from the
freezer and cut into slices.

*Photograph opposite
(bottom)*

Sicilian Cassata
Cassata alla Siciliana

Serves 12
Preparation time: 1½ hours
530 kcal

For the cake mixture:

5 eggs, separated

a pinch of salt

juice of ½ lemon

100 g/4 oz/½ cup sugar

10 ml/2 tsp grated lemon rind

10 ml/2 tsp grated orange rind

10 ml/2 tsp vanilla essence

100 g/4 oz/1 cup plain flour

a pinch of baking powder

butter for greasing

For the filling:

700 g/1 lb Ricotta cheese

200 g/7 oz/1¾ cups sugar

10 ml/2 tsp vanilla essence

150 ml/¼ pt/⅔ cup orange liqueur

100 g/4 oz chocolate chips

100 g/4 oz chopped mixed peel

50 g/2 oz/¼ cup glacé cherries, chopped

50 g/2 oz/½ cup walnuts, chopped

50 g/2 oz/⅓ cup raisins soaked in rum

225 g/8 oz chocolate cake covering

sweetened whipped cream

candied fruit to taste

1 Beat the egg whites with a little salt and lemon juice until stiff. Preheat the oven to 180°C/350°F/gas mark 4.

2 Whisk the egg yolks, with the sugar until thick and foamy. Carefully mix in the lemon and orange rind with the vanilla essence.

3 Sieve the flour with the baking powder and fold into the egg yolk mixture with a metal spoon.

4 Gently fold in the beaten egg whites.

5 Grease a 20 cm/8 in spring-form tin and fill with cake mixture. Bake for 20 to 25 minutes until well risen and golden. Remove from the oven and leave to cool.

6 Cut the cake horizontally into four thin layers.

7 To make the filling, mix the Ricotta, sugar, vanilla essence, orange liqueur and chocolate chips in a bowl until smooth. Stir in the peel, glacé cherries and walnuts. Fold in the rum-soaked raisins.

8 Spread one-third of the mixture on to each of the three cake layers, lay them on top of each other and cover with the fourth layer.

9 Cover the cake with the liquid chocolate covering, leave to set then garnish the cake with cream and fruit.

Ricotta Flapjacks
Biscotti di Ricotta

Serves 4
Preparation time: 1 hour
655 kcal

400 g/14 oz Ricotta cheese
225 g/7 oz/2 cups plain flour
2 eggs
10 ml/2 tsp vanilla essence
25 g/1 oz/1/4 cup blanched almonds, chopped
25 g/1 oz/1/4 cup pistachio nuts
75 g/3 oz/1/2 cup raisins soaked in rum
a few drops of orange liqueur
sugar to taste
oil for frying
90 ml/6 tbsp honey

1 Put the Ricotta into a bowl and work to a dough with the flour, eggs, vanilla essence, almonds, pistachios and raisins.
2 Flavour the dough with a little orange liqueur and add sugar according to taste. Shape into flattish cakes.
3 Heat the oil in a deep frying pan and gently lower in the cakes. Fry until golden brown. Remove from the pan and drain well. Spread with honey and serve hot.

Photograph opposite (top)

St Joseph's Doughnuts
Binge di San Giuseppe

Serves 4
Preparation time: 1 hour
360 kcal

a pinch of salt
100 g/4 oz/1/2 cup icing sugar
2 vanilla pods
10 ml/2 tsp grated lemon rind
juice of 1 lemon
10 ml/2 tsp grated orange rind
50 g/2 oz/1/4 cup butter
100 g/4 oz/1 cup plain flour
4 eggs
a good pinch of baking powder
oil for frying
20 ml/4 tsp cinnamon

1 Bring 300 ml/1/2 pt/1 1/4 cups of water to the boil. Add the salt, 10 ml/2 tsp of sugar, the flesh scraped from the vanilla pods, the lemon rind, lemon juice, orange rind and the butter.
2 Add the flour in one go and stir briskly with a wooden spoon until the mixture forms a ball in the pan, leaving the sides clean. Cool to lukewarm.
3 Beat the eggs into the mixture one after another then add baking powder. Using a teaspoon, make little dumplings of the dough and deep-fry them in hot oil.

4 Remove the doughnuts and leave to drain. Mix the cinnamon with the rest of the sugar and use to coat doughnuts. Serve hot or warm.

Photograph opposite (centre)

Apron Doughnuts
Chiacchiere

Serves 4
Preparation time: 1 hour
685 kcal

450 g/1 lb/4 cups plain flour
100 g/4 oz/1/2 cup sugar
10 ml/2 tsp vanilla essence
10 ml/2 tsp grated orange rind
3 eggs, beaten
150 ml/1/4 pt/2/3 cup orange liqueur
oil for frying
icing sugar for sprinkling

1 Put the flour into a bowl. Add the sugar, vanilla essence and orange rind.
2 Add the eggs and the orange liqueur and knead to a firm dough.
3 Knead once more until smooth then roll out on a floured board to about 1 cm/1/2 in thickness.
4 Cut little balls or bows out of the dough and deep-fry until golden.
5 Remove from the pan, drain well, sprinkle with icing sugar and leave to cool a little before serving.

Photograph opposite (bottom)

Index of Recipes

Italian-English Glossary

Use this to help you when you visit Italian restaurants.

Italian	English	Italian	English	Italian	English
aceto	– vinegar	fungo	– mushroom	pera	– pear
aglio	– garlic			pesca	– peach
albicocca	– apricot	gelato	– ice cream	pesce	– fish
anguilla	– eel			piatto di	– egg dish
aragosta	– lobster	latte	– milk	uova	
arrosto	– roast			pollo	– chicken
		maiale	– pork	pomodoro	– tomato
biscotto	– biscuit	manzo	– beef	proscuitto	– cured ham
brodo di	– chicken	mela	– apple		
pollo	broth/stock	melanzana	– aubergine	ricotta	– cheese
budino	– pudding	miele	– honey		similar to
burro	– butter	minestra,	– soup		quark or
		brodo			fromage
calamaro	– squid	minestra di	– vegetable		frais
carne	– meat	verdura	soup	risco	– rice
carota	– carrot				
cavolo	– cabbage	noce	– nut	saccarina	– sweetener
cetriolo	– cucumber			spezzatino	– goulash
ciliegia	– cherry	olio	– oil	di carne	
cioccolata	– chocolate				
contorno di	– vegetable	pane	– bread	torta	– gâteau
verdura	side dish	panino	– bread roll	trota	– trout
		panna	– cream		
dolce	– sweet	pasta	– noodles	verdura	– vegetable
	dessert	paste	– pastries		
		pastina in	– noodle	zucca	– pumpkin
fegato	– liver	brodo	soup	zucchero	– sugar
formaggio	– cheese	peperone	– red or	zuppa di	– fish soup
frutta	– fruit		green	pesce	
			peppers		

foulsham
Yeovil Road, Slough, Berkshire, SL1 4JH

ISBN 0-572-01707-3

This English language edition copyright ©
1992 W. Foulsham & Co. Ltd
Originally published by Falken-Verlag,
GmbH, Niedernhausen TS, Germany
Photographs copyright © Falken-Verlag

All rights reserved.
The Copyright Act (1956) prohibits (subject
to certain very limited exceptions) the
making of copies of any copyright work or
of a substantial part of such a work,
including the making of copies by
photocopying or similar process. Written
permission to make a copy or copies must
therefore normally be obtained from the
publisher in advance. It is advisable also to
consult the publisher if in any doubt as to
the legality of any copying which is to be
undertaken.

Printed in Portugal